Loving Who I Am
Inside & Out
For Women Who Value Their Worth

By Stephanie L. McKenny

Loving Who I Am

Inside & Out

For Women Who Value Their Worth

ISBN: 978-0-9961018-2-0

Copyright © 2018 ~ J & J Publishing Company

A self-publishing company owned by

Stephanie L. McKenny

Dedication

I dedicate this book in the loving memory of my mother,

Marian L. Garrett

(1934-2005)

Loving Who I Am

Contents

Chapter 1 You Better Recognize   7

Chapter 2 Who Validates You?   31

Chapter 3 What Are You Thinking?   39

Chapter 4 Wounds & Scars   45

Chapter 5 Blast from the Past   59

Chapter 6 Forgiveness   81

Chapter 7 Words You Say & Hear   85

Chapter 8 Appearances   99

Chapter 9 Your Purpose   103

        Final Words   111

        About the Author   113

Chapter 1: You Better Recognize

Hey, beautiful Lady! Yes, I'm talking about you. Listen, your beauty far exceeds your outward appearance because your beauty runs deeper than that. It springs up from within. In case you didn't know or maybe no one has ever told you, but you are not only beautiful, you are also a valuable woman. Your Creator was very persistent about you existing right now in this moment of time. Your life is so significant and it has meaning beyond what you can even imagine. You are a woman of great influence and power. Please understand that by me just writing this to you is simply not enough. You must love who you are right now and believe it for yourself. This belief must resonate deep within your soul in order to combat anything that tries to suggest to you otherwise.

One of the keys to living life to the fullest is when you can recognize your value and worth. Doing so creates so many positive outcomes for you. You see, when you recognize your value you are less prone to settle for anything less than the best for your life because you know you deserve it. I can remember a saying coming up, "You better recognize." It was a saying that simply meant that you better recognize who I am or what I'm capable of doing. It clearly expressed to others not to even doubt you because you had whatever it took to make things happen. So when it comes to loving who you are right now and knowing your value....you better recognize!

I'm sure throughout the course of your life; you have experienced some unpleasant situations, heard some negativity in your life concerning you and/or have felt unworthy at some point in your life. Even though this may very well be part of your truth, it doesn't mean that your story ends there. You are still here, you are still strong and you are indeed a valuable woman. The minute you begin to recognize your value for yourself, it then becomes recognizable to those around you. There are some people who already see your value. They recognize your gifts and abilities and they make every effort to help you see it. Gravitate to those who see your value and believe in where you are going in life. These people will aid you in your own recognition of your value. It's always good to have people that believe in you in your life, but ultimately YOU must see your worth for yourself. Loving who you are right now is so important. Don't concern yourself about the flaws in your life because we all have them. Your flaws should not be your focus. Shift your mind from that. Your focus should be on recognizing your value, identifying your divine assignment and experiencing the abundant life promised to you.

Knowing and recognizing your value has everything to do with how you see yourself. What matters the most is how you think of yourself and what you truly feel about yourself. Your self-esteem plays a prominent part in your life. It aids you in your thinking, your actions and the connections you will make in your life. This can influence you negatively or positively depending upon where you are in your level of self-worth.

One of the definitions of self-esteem is having confidence in one's own worth and abilities. It's a feeling of having respect for yourself and your abilities. This definition clearly describes a person who has a healthy self-esteem. When you possess respect and confidence for yourself, your worth and your abilities, it exudes out of you the very essence of feeling good about who you are. When you have a healthy self-esteem, you know who you are and are aware of the direction for your life. Having a healthy self-esteem makes it difficult for you to think negatively about yourself and/or your abilities. However, when a person has low self-esteem, it creates negativity to flow in their thought life, their actions, their choices and many others areas of their life. The effects of either, high or low self-esteem can affect and even change a person's life.

Initially, I had no idea what self-esteem was nor did I know the impact it made on how I felt about myself or the choices I would make and the people I would connect with. As I grew to understand this concept, I realized that I suffered from low self-esteem. Not totally sure as to how it all began to develop in me, but it did exist. However, as time progressed and as I began to dig deep within, I gathered information that helped me to see how the seed was planted in my heart. It began with my past mistakes as a young teenager and the shame I felt I brought to my family because of my poor choices. Because of this, I can recall always longing for the approval of my parents, my dad especially. I wanted to please him. I wanted him to be proud of me. I wanted to be good enough, but because I had a child as a teenager those negative seeds were planted and my level of self-esteem decreased.

Looking back now, after getting past all those feelings and maturing, I can remember receiving positive prophecies about God using me to preach, facilitate conferences and that I would write books. My thoughts then were that's not really going to happen is it? Not in a million years, I thought. Little did I know I would do exactly that and more. I can remember thinking that there was no way I was getting up before people to say anything. I didn't feel as though I was good enough. I can remember feeling nervous and thinking that I would mess up. There are still times when those feelings of not being good enough try to resurface. When they do, the Holy Spirit kindly reminds me that I am good enough and that God has placed some great things inside of me that I've got to release to others. I knew there was no way I could help others properly if I still had this issue of not loving and valuing myself appropriately.

I didn't want my hurt, shame and guilt to trickle down to the next woman. I wanted to be healed because I realized that being healed was far better than being broken. This is exactly where God wants you to be, healed and not broken. There is too much at stake and too many great things for you to see and do. Whether you go after things or not is a direct reflection of how you feel about yourself overall. Loving who you are is truly important.

After having my experiences of unhealthy relationships, I realized something had to change in me from the inside out. I had to begin to feel good about me. So I began to get in God's Word and began speaking positive words into my life. I had to change my inner circle and surround myself with people that believed in me, loved me and were in agreement with where I was going in life.

I finally realized that the reason why the enemy was trying so hard to get me to underestimate myself is because he had a slight indication that God had some great things in store for my life and that my life was connected to other lives that I would help.

This too could be happening to you. There are outside influences (many times we use the term our adversary) that desperately want to distract you by using your past failures, the hurt, the pain, disappointments of the past or having feelings of not being good enough. Those negative outside influences will even have you feeling bad about not being able to measure up to the opinions of others.

First of all, you need to understand that you don't have to measure up to anyone else's opinion. The thoughts and opinions that you have of yourself is what matters the most. Negative influences and distractions are set out on purpose to block you from moving forward in life. However, you can make the decision today to change the course that is being set to derail you. It begins with loving who you are right now. I can't emphasis enough how important this is. When we don't love ourselves appropriately it will manifest in our behaviors, our actions, our words, how we treat ourselves and how we allow others to treat us.

> What are some of the points in these paragraphs that stand out to you?

_____

_____

_____

_____

_____

_____

_____

➢ How will the points you listed help to change your thinking and your actions?

_____

_____

_____

_____

_____

_____

The purpose of this section of the book is to help you become aware of how you feel about yourself. What are some of the words you would use to describe you?

_____

_____

_____

_____

_____

There are many ways that we reveal to ourselves about how we feel about who we are. We also show others how we feel about who we are by our overall conduct. It is displayed in how we treat ourselves and how we allow others to treat us. So, the question is how do you feel about yourself?

_____

_____

_____

After you've answered this question, take the time to write at least five (5) reasons that caused you to come to that conclusion.

_____

_____

_____

_____

_____

> What were some of the lies (negative and derogatory words) you heard said about who you are?

_____

_____

_____

_____

_____

> How have those words affected you now?

_____

_____

_____

_____

_____

➤ What are some statements of truth that you can write about yourself to combat the lies you have heard? Take the time to speak positive words over your life. Words that will help to edify who you are.

_____

_____

_____

_____

_____

_____

You must love yourself first before you can effectively love anyone else in your life. Can you honestly say that you love yourself? Answering this question truthfully can help you recognize if you are going to be able to love others in a healthy way. The scripture even tells us to love our neighbor as we love ourselves (Matthew 22:39). The issue behind us not properly loving our neighbor is because we don't fully love ourselves. We must love who we are. We must love who we are right now, not who we will become. You are good enough right now.

I know you might have heard differently in the past, but today is a fresh start at re-launching the new you. Loving who you are now begins the healing process. *Your bad behaviors, poor choices and experiences are not a totality of who you are.* These things are PART of you and your life experiences, but they do not consist of who you are entirely. While you still have breath in your body, you have the power to make the necessary changes to become a better person, which can begin from the inside out.

TREATING YOURSELF

How do you treat yourself? Do you put others before you? Sometimes this can be difficult for women who have children and/or a spouse because we are nurturers by nature and we always try to find a way to make it right for others, but somehow shortchange ourselves.

When we shortchange ourselves, we are actually saying that we are not good enough or important enough to tend to. Are you important? Of course you are. If you are shortchanging yourself for the sake of others, then you must take the time to evaluate this behavior and figure out why you do this. In your evaluation of this, you must search your heart for the truth even if it's something you really don't want to face. As you search within, eradicate the thoughts that come to your mind that make you feel "guilty" about doing something special for you on a consistent basis. Those feelings of guilt come from a source of negativity planted in your heart at some point in your life. Let those feelings go immediately. Embrace the fact that it's okay to do something special for you just because you want to and because you deserve it.

When you shortchange yourself, this will only cause you to experience wear and tear on your overall (mentally, physically and emotionally) being. This will affect everything around you. When you empty out your fuel tank for others and never fill back up, you will soon realize there will be no fuel for yourself. Allowing yourself to do things that make you feel good is not being selfish, but this shows you and others that you value yourself.

➤ Do you personally feel that you shortchange yourself? If so, how?

_____

_____

_____

_____

_____

_____

➤ If so, why do you do this? Share the emotions you feel.

_____

_____

_____

_____

_____

_____

➤ If you've realized that you've short changed yourself in the past, what will you now do differently?

_____

_____

_____

_____

_____

When you love yourself and make yourself a priority, it will become evident in your overall actions. It will attract the right people into your life. The atmosphere responds to what we send out to it. When we truly love ourselves it will cause us to practice self-care, which is essential. When you love and take care of yourself, you will be able to help yourself and others. You really are important.

Taking care of yourself involves many factors. It affects your spirit, soul and body. Self-care for your spirit (Proverbs 18:14 – "The spirit of a man will sustain his infirmity; but a wounded spirit who can bear?") involves taking time for your own personal spiritual development. When your spirit is strong, you will be strong. As the scripture declares, you will be strong even in the midst of infirmity (tough times, sickness etc.) because your spirit will sustain you. Developing your spiritual awareness and growth is important. This means you will need to make time to meditate on God's Word and to pray to obtain clear direction for your life.

Self-care for your soul (mind, will and emotions) involves making sure that you are doing things that give you peace of mind. Stimulate your mind so that you can think clearly and make proper decisions. Learning to balance and control your emotions is an attribute of someone who values themselves and others. You don't want to be a person that is easily moved by your emotions. Feelings and emotions can change at any given time, so it's important to learn to balance them.

Self-care for your body consists of eating the right things; practicing a proper diet and making sure that your body remains active (exercising) to keep it operating at its optimum level.

➤ Name some things that you specifically do for yourself as a treat to you.

_____

_____

_____

_____

_____

➤ What have you done for YOU lately?

_____

_____

_____

_____

➤ Write down three (3) things that would really make YOU feel good.

_____

_____

_____

_____

HOW DO OTHERS TREAT YOU?

Sometimes we may wonder why people treat us the way they do, especially if they are treating us unfairly. It's because we actually teach people how we want to be treated based on how we treat ourselves. How you treat yourself is a direct reflection of how you feel about yourself. Think of it as being your self-esteem screaming out to others how you value or disvalue who you are. If you don't take care of yourself and your overall well-being, it speaks volumes to others that it really doesn't matter if they treat you right or not. I can't emphasize enough how important it is to embrace a healthy self-esteem and to dismantle the unhealthy one.

We also teach people how to treat us based on how we allow them to treat us. Your overall interactions with people teach them how to treat you. You have the power to set the rules of appropriate treatment from day one. I hate to say this, but I have to, sometimes you can't point the blame at the other person for treating you poorly. They are only treating you like that because you have possibly allowed them to treat you that way. Their behavior may not be appropriate or acceptable, but you can't allow their behavior to cause you to accept what they are dishing out. You deserve to be treated right. You deserve to be loved. So don't allow anyone to mistreat you in any way. Teach them to treat you right. You must have standards of how you want to be treated; live by them and make sure others learn them as well.

When it comes to interacting in a relationship with a man, you are the woman in the relationship and you really have the power when it comes to determining how a man will treat you. He follows your lead. Now he may make the suggestion, but you have the power to choose. It's the same in any other relationship that consists with friends, business associates and/or ministry affiliation; you set the standard of how you want to be treated with those who enter your life. When you notice that people don't recognize your value, don't waste your time trying to prove to them that you are a valuable woman. If they can't recognize that you have so much to offer the ministry, the business or the relationship, don't spend much time trying to convince them. Either they'll catch it later or they will miss out on it all together. Nevertheless, know that you have value and your life has purpose and meaning. Move forward and don't look back.

➢ What are some of the points in these paragraphs that stand out to you?

_____

_____

_____

_____

_____

_____

➢ How will these points change your thinking and/or actions

_____

_____

_____

_____

_____

HOW DO YOU TREAT PEOPLE?

There is another question to consider when it comes to the treatment of other people in your life. How do you treat other people? Sometimes how we feel about ourselves is projected onto another. If we have feelings of not being good enough, we will project those same feelings onto others without even realizing it. For example, if you are very critical of yourself, you find it hard to compliment yourself and others. You tend to be more critical to another because you're critical on yourself. The negativity has formed in your mindset and it has no choice, but to escape out in the form of your words. The scriptures tell us that out of the abundance of the heart, the mouth will speak.

When someone else gives you a compliment, you will find in some way to see fault in it. Or you will find some way not to accept it at all. For example, someone could say to you, "Your dress looks beautiful. It really looks good on you." And your response is, "Oh, this old thing. I had it for a long time. I really never liked how I look in it, but I threw it on." What??? Why couldn't you just say, "Thank you." The negative response is a direct result of what you may be feeling about yourself inwardly. That behavior is one of the indications that you may have an issue with self-esteem.

If you don't feel good enough, then you will in some way find fault in another person to project that they are not good enough either. If you have been criticized by others for a specific length of time, you will soon find yourself being critical to others. We often hear people say, "Hurt people; hurt people." I agree with this saying because no one can properly love themselves or others for that matter when they are filled with hurt, bitterness and frustration. This type of behavior has to be uprooted from your thinking, your words and your actions. Any personal baggage that you may still be carrying from the past will weigh you down and cause you to treat people inappropriately. This is why it's essential to get rid of the emotional baggage. The healing process must begin from the inside out so that you can properly love you and others.

When you are dealing with issues of low self-esteem and insecurities, you will even find it difficult to compliment another person. People with low self-esteem and insecurities feel as though complimenting another person takes away from who they are. Giving a compliment to another will not only encourage another person, but it shows that you are confident in who you are. No one's abilities, looks or their position should cause you to feel jealous or threatened in any way. You have great strengths and abilities that are right at your fingertips. Focus on what you're doing and where you want to go and you won't have time to be consumed with jealousy or insecurities by someone else's achievements.

> What are your feelings on how you treat other people?

_____

_____

_____

> What do you think you can do better when it comes to treating people fairly in your life?

_____

_____

_____

_____

➢ Give a compliment to another person daily for the next 10 days. How did it make the other person feel? How did it make you feel?

_____

_____

_____

_____

After reading through this chapter, I hope that you see the importance of making sure you recognize your value so that you can treat yourself right. Not only treating you right is essential, but making sure that others treat you right as well. Loving who you are right now is the pivotal point that dictates the cycle of how things will flow in many areas of your life. I can't emphasize enough that you are good enough....you better recognize!

"THIS IS WHAT I SEE WHEN I LOOK AT ME"

ACTIVITY: WRITE THE WORDS THAT YOU FEEL REFLECT WHO YOU ARE. HOW WOULD YOU DESCRIBE YOURSELF?

ACTIVITY: Write down 5 positive things about you and post it on a wall where you can see it.

1._____

2._____

3._____

4. _____

5._____

"I AM MY OWN FAN – LOVING WHO I AM
INSIDE AND OUT"

"10 Ways to Rebuild Self-Esteem"

1. Pray and meditate on God's Word.
2. Write down some positive things about yourself.
3. Write down some things that you have accomplished.
4. Speak positive words over your life on a daily basis. Make positive declarations.
5. Examine your inner circle. Make sure the people around you are building you up and not tearing you down. Be around people who celebrate you and not just tolerate you.
6. Forgive yourself from past failures and hurts.
7. Forgive others. I know this may be easier said than done, but it must be done in order for you to move forward. When you don't forgive, you give that person power over you. Release yourself and forgive.
8. Think positively. How you feel about yourself begins with your own thoughts. It's not what others think about you, what matters the most is how you think of yourself. Your thoughts affect your actions and your actions affect your destiny.
9. Read motivational books; listen to motivational CDs that will remind you of how valuable you are.
10. Celebrate your achievements whether they are big or small.

Chapter 2: Who Validates You?

I'm not sure if you remember the story of *Snow White*, but in the story, the wicked queen had this routine of asking the mirror if she was the fairest of them all. This wicked queen was seeking validation. Her intentions were to seek affirmation of her beauty and worth. She was already a queen, but for some reason she felt the need to ask the mirror who was the fairest of them all.

It's interesting that it was a mirror that she looked at. Many of us have a mirror before us; not necessarily a physical mirror, but there is an image that we view on a daily basis that helps us to determine whether we are worthy enough. That mirror is within us. The mirror within us reflects how we feel about ourselves. This reflection shines to all that see you. It's clearly displayed by your actions, your behavior and your words. Keep in mind that the mirror shows everything about you, your beauty, your scars and your flaws. You may not like the scars and the flaws, but this doesn't have to put a limitation on you. You have the capability of being and doing whatever you desire. The important thing to remember is that you must love yourself and be confident in who you are. You can always move beyond your flaws, mistakes and opinions of others. Your very existence is more than enough validation that your life is significant and you have purpose.

Your mirror within, the image you have of yourself is the compass that guides you. It directs you on how you will maneuver in life. This is why it's important to value yourself and allow God's Word to validate and affirm who you are. Our first initial image came from God. We were created in His image and likeness (Genesis 1:26-27). Can I give you heads up on something? You really have it going on more than you realize. You were good enough from the beginning and you still are good enough now.

Sometimes it's that woman on the inside (inner woman) that often finds it difficult to accept that she's good enough. The inner woman sometimes struggles with remembering that God has placed and developed greatness within her (YOU!). God has never made junk because everything God made was good and that includes you too. You are His created masterpiece. Sometimes we allow our experiences to cause us to think less of ourselves and before we know it we've allowed our own self-sabotaging thoughts to cause us to overlook the image we've been created from. If that's been your issue, don't allow it to be your issue from this day forward. Reflect on the image of God. Reflect on what He says about you in His Word. Use the Word of God as your mirror, reflect on it, and conform to the image revealed through it.

The wicked queen in *Snow White* was looking for the mirror to respond to her. She was looking for another person's opinion to determine her worth. This is not something you should get accustomed to doing. Other people's opinion of you is only a limited view of who you are. Sometimes when we don't recognize our worth, we tend to become *dependent* upon the opinions and affirmations of others to determine the validity of our worth. The opinions of people that we hold in high esteem tend to carry weight in how we see ourselves. However, their opinion is not as important as the opinion you have of yourself. Their opinion has limitations. You have to see yourself as beautiful, worthy, good enough and important. You have to know this for yourself because as you know, everyone is not going to affirm or validate you.

You have to determine now that you will be okay with or without the validation. And you will. You will be fine with or without the validation of others.

➤ Do you feel as though you need validation in order to determine how you feel about yourself?

_____

_____

_____

➤ What stood out to you in these paragraphs?

_____

_____

_____

_____

➤ How did it impact you?

_____

_____

_____

➤ What will you do with this information now that you have it?

_____

_____

_____

_____

Don't get me wrong, its fine to receive validation. It is a source of encouragement when it comes. At some point in our lives, we have received it and we have longed for it when it didn't exist. Consider your experience with validation as you ponder these questions.

➢ Who validates you?

_____

_____

_____

➢ Who is the person that makes you feel worthy? There is someone or at least there should be at least one person who affirms you.

_____

_____

_____

_____

➢ What are some of the things that they share with you to affirm who you are?

_____

_____

_____

_____

_____

_____

➢ Do you feel as though you have become dependent upon the need for this validation? If so, why?

_____

_____

_____

_____

_____

_____

Another thing to consider when it comes to validation is that some of us have never received validation and/or affirmation when we needed it. Sometimes not receiving the validation was dated all the way back to our childhood. Sometimes we may wonder why people are drawn to the need for validation. This could very well be because it wasn't received. People that constantly look for validation may appear needy, always looking for approval or acceptance of others.

➢ Who was it that didn't give you the validation you needed or deserved? Was it your Father? Was it your Mother? Was it your grandparents?

_____

_____

_____

_____

_____

_____

If there was someone in your life that didn't validate you, unfortunately you may very well go through life looking for affirmation and validation. The lack of validation could cause you to long to quench the thirst of feeling whether you are good enough. You may do this consciously or subconsciously. If you didn't receive it earlier on in life, you will look for it. You will long for it and sometimes that longing leads you to the strangest places. Some of those places end up being somewhere you wish you would've never gone. Sometimes it creates connections with people that are not healthy for you. This is why it's so important to know who you are; believe in you and see yourself as being worthy. Loving who you are no matter what will help you to dissipate that quench, that longing for acceptance and validation.

➢ Who are the people that you need to have a conversation with to bring resolution to your lack of validation?

_____

_____

_____

➢ If you're unable to have that conversation with that individual or individuals, will you be able to move forward? How will you do it?

_____

_____

_____

_____

Even though we all may need some form of validation, we shouldn't allow ourselves to become dependent upon it. Be careful about becoming dependent upon others to affirm and/or validate who you are. You must have the drive and the passion to go after your goals. You must make the first step in loving who you are right now; even if you're not happy with some of your experiences. You must think positively about yourself and begin to make daily affirmations over your life to encourage yourself. You are good enough and your life is significant.

ACTIVITY ZONE:
> **Activity:** Write a letter to the person that did not properly validate you. Express how you felt about it then and how you feel about it now. Express your forgiveness for their actions or lack thereof.
> **Activity:** The "Empty Chair" – Share what you want to say to that person as if they were actually sitting in that chair across from you.
> **Activity:** Create your own affirmation and read it daily.

Chapter 3: What Are You Thinking?

What do you really think about yourself? Be honest. Take a moment to think about that. Whether you realize it or not, how you think about yourself plays an intricate part of how things are in your life right now. You thought about it, you acted upon and the results manifested.

Your thoughts are powerful. It's the thoughts you have on a daily basis that determine your overall mood, actions and behavior. Your thoughts reveal your feelings about everything that pertains to you. Thoughts that you have about yourself, other people and the situations you face will dictate your actions. Take a moment and think about some of your past behaviors. As you ponder on this, you will find that it was your thoughts about that particular situation that made you say what you said and do what you did.

Your thought process, which began its formulation in your childhood, has governed your decision making, your selection of friends and the kind of treatment you will and will not accept from others. What you allow to filter into your spirit, to be planted in your thought life affects many facets of your life. This is why it's so important for you to guard your heart, guard your thought life attentively. Stand on guard like a watchman on the wall to monitor what you allow to enter into your heart. Keep in mind that every suggested thought is not meant to be carried out or even entertained. Filter out the negativity immediately. Your thoughts coupled with your actions affect your destiny so monitor your thoughts closely because it starts there.

There are some people who are stuck in various areas of their life simply because of their overall thinking. They are what I consider to be stuck in their thoughts. They are moving through life, but there is no real progress. They continue in the same routine cycle hoping for a change. However, a missing piece of information that has the ability to set them free does not exist in their thought process. Exposure to new information can elevate your thinking. Sometimes all we need is a new perspective on things to generate a new way of thinking.

Maybe this has been something that has happened to you or is happening now. When you consider people who are stuck in their thoughts, they may really desire to move forward in life, but there is something in their thoughts that paralyzes them. Sometimes they are or are not aware of this. Some people are stuck and don't realize they're stuck until they are exposed to a different way of doing things. When they finally come to an "aha" moment, they recognize that their way of thinking has ensnared them for so long.

Sometimes people are stuck in their thoughts because they don't feel good about themselves. They could be stuck because of the negative words that someone spoke into their lives. This could have happened in their childhood or even as an adult. It could be that they don't believe in themselves. It could be that they are suspicious about everyone and fearful to move forward. These thoughts cause them to become stuck in their thoughts.

If this is you, you must identify and acknowledge that you are stuck. You must then be open to allow the Holy Spirit to heal and guide you. Be open to receive information that can liberate your way of thinking so you can move progressively forward in life.

➢ Do you feel stuck? If you do, what do you feel has caused you to be this way?

_____

_____

_____

Sometimes the way we see things may not necessarily be the only way to see it. This causes us to become stuck in our ways because our thoughts or our perception of something has remained the same. As mentioned earlier, sometimes new insight, a different perspective and/or new information can cause us to expand in our thinking and upgrade our thought processing. A change in thoughts can change your life when those thoughts are properly implemented.

➢ Have you ever taken the time to think about what you think about on a daily basis? Take a minute to write down some of those daily thoughts you have.

_____

_____

_____

_____

Your thoughts formulate energy that projects from you. Your thoughts cause things to attract themselves to you. It really depends on what kind of thoughts you are having on a daily basis that will determine what will be attracted to you. You pull to you what you think and believe within. A change in your thinking will change your behaviors. Your change in your thinking can cause greater things to be attracted to you. If you want things to become different in your life, it will begin from within. The change has to begin in you through your thought life first.

YOUR THOUGHTS MATTER

Believe it or not, one of the ways that your self-esteem is formulated is based on your own thought life. We are what we think we are. Proverbs 23:7a *"For as he thinketh in his heart, so is he:"* This scripture lets us know what we think about ourselves is who we are. What we think we are is who we will become. Your thoughts about you are essential in how you will interact on a daily basis. Your thoughts determine your overall actions because what we think about the most is what we will become and what we will do. If you think you're going to make it and achieve your goals; nine times out of ten you most likely will. If you think you're a failure, then that energy released from your thoughts, will cause opposition to gravitate to you to create the scenarios to fail. Your thoughts matter. They determine how you genuinely feel about yourself. Your thoughts can very well motivate you to reach for your dreams or goals you desire to accomplish. Your thoughts also have the ability to cause you to talk yourself out of reaching your dreams too. Be mindful of what you're thinking about so that your thinking doesn't limit your abilities.

Sometimes people can't move forward in life because they can't move past the words that someone has spoken over their lives. Those words have a tendency to play so conveniently in your mind at the strangest times. They sound like a scratched CD that continues to repeat over and over again when it gets to the scratched area on the CD. Sometimes you can clean the CD and it will play smoothly. Sometimes you will have to clean up and modify your way of thinking to get the best out of your life. Then there are the times when that scratched CD is no longer any good and you have to throw it away. This is what you have to do with negative and self-sabotaging thoughts that try to overtake you. You have to eradicate those negative thoughts so you can move on with your life the way God intended it to be.

> ➤ Are you stuck because of some of the things people said to you? If so, share them here.

_____

_____

_____

_____

> ➤ Who was the person that said these things to you? How does it make you feel now?

_____

_____

_____

_____

> ➤ What were some specific incidents in your life that helped to formulate your way of thinking about yourself?

_____

_____

_____

Oftentimes, the thoughts about ourselves can come from words we heard others say about us, what we've been saying to ourselves and how we think/feel about ourselves. Our thoughts sometimes form from the experiences we've had and what we have witnessed. Your behavior "actions" towards a person or situation is a mere reflection of your inner thoughts. We usually act upon our thoughts.

Your overall thoughts about yourself will help in determining whether you go after your goals, dreams and aspirations. Your perception is your reality. If you think you are able to go after your dreams, you will do it. You must consider that there will be opposition that you may face, but you can't allow yourself to get stuck there. You must move beyond it all. Moving beyond initially begins with your thoughts.

There is a reason why we perceive things to be as they are. You may have to ask yourself how you began to think the way you do about yourself. When did all this come about? There are several reasons why you may have a certain perception of yourself; whether it's positive or negative. The key is to identify how it began and then make every effort to plant a new way of thinking so as to uproot any negative thought processing. A new way of thinking has the ability to change your entire life from what it is right now. You hold the keys for change to take place in your life through your very own thoughts. Begin today by loving who you are, valuing yourself and believing in your destiny....in your thoughts.

Chapter 4: Wounds & Scars

*(Excerpt from Clutch Your Pearls, Girl! – Sister Wisdom to Protect Your Heart
by Stephanie L. McKenny)*

Remember when you were a little girl and you fell down for the first time? You cried and then ran to your mother in hopes that she would make you feel better. She would grab you, give you a hug to calm you down and then begin working on your bruise. She would clean it, put some first-aid ointment on it and cover it with a bandage. From that point on, the healing process began.

As you can see, covering the wound with a bandage is the initial remedy. The number of days the wound should be covered is determined by the severity of the wound itself. Initially, the bandages are applied so the wound won't be hit again, which could create a more serious injury or additional pain. No one wants to be hit again especially if the wound hasn't completely healed; yet, the bandages were not meant to remain on the wound forever.

The analogy mentioned above is what takes place when we are wounded physically; however, the wounds I am referring to are the disappointments you've encountered, the negative words spoken in your ears that still linger in your spirit, the emotional scars from life experiences and possibly the physical scars from abusive relationships.

Many of us have handled our hurting experiences by covering them up, hoping that in time we would heal; needless to say, some of us continued to be hit over and over again with the same kind of hurt. In response to never wanting to hurt again, we built a wall around us, put our masks on and swept it all under the rug without totally healing from the emotional scars that were left behind.

Healing was in view, but forgiving was totally out of the question.

> What are some experiences you've had that you still try to cover up?

_____

_____

_____

_____

> Has covering it up helped your healing process or delayed it? How so?

_____

_____

_____

_____

_____

When we have experienced being hurt by someone we love, we find it difficult, at times to heal, much less forgive. The length of time for the healing process is determined by the severity of the hurt, the individual that hurt you and how long the hurtful experience took place. Sometimes we think we've been healed, but in actuality we've allowed ourselves to suppress it in our subconscious. We actually made it go away in our mind. Of course we later realized, when we've been "hit again" with the same kind of hurt or hurt by the same person, that the wound was never really completely healed in the first place. We just packed it down and covered it up.

It's similar to when someone brings up an old incident (an old boyfriend, a childhood experience or a bad separation or divorce). You are quick to say, "I'm fine. I don't even think about it anymore." And, as those words are leaving your mouth, your insides are still cringing with the feelings of that old hurt. You realize then that you really haven't quite gotten over what they did to you. If you can't talk about it or deal with others discussing it, then it's possible you still need to be healed from it.

> ➤ Are there some experiences that you still find difficult to talk about? Name one that comes to mind.

_____

_____

_____

_____

_____

> ➤ Take a moment to journal some of your thoughts about those experiences.

_____

_____

_____

_____

_____

_____

I can remember a tough time in my life when I was deeply hurt by someone I loved. They hurt me continually on and off for years, but I packed it down and kept it covered and tried to convince myself daily that it really didn't bother me anymore. As far as I was concerned, I was over it.

In the beginning, when the hurt first occurred, moving towards forgiveness was a struggle for me because I felt justified for not letting it all go. I held it for years, kept it covered so no one could see my hurt or the bitterness that had begun to set in my heart. Soon I noticed that my love for this person began to change; it grew cold. Nevertheless, I continued to go to church and continued to follow my daily routines. As the Word of God kept coming forth from the pulpit concerning forgiveness, the wall I had built so perfectly around me began to crumble down. After hearing the Word, I felt exposed before the Lord. I realized then that I had to forgive. Only at that point, could God mend my heart and take me through the healing process. I got through by being honest with God about how I felt concerning this situation, hearing His Word and applying what I heard in my life. I was able to forgive and love that person again.

> Has it been a struggle for you to forgive someone? Why has it been a struggle?

_____

_____

_____

_____

_____

_____

Part of your healing will begin when you are totally honest with yourself and with God. You have to confront those emotional wounds and allow God to uproot all that stuff that was never planted by Him in the first place. Not dealing with it will never heal it. Healing is a process. Some wounds have a way of healing on their own; while others take more time and require more of our effort. No matter how much time is required for you to heal emotionally, go after your healing because being healed is far better than being broken. Being broken is not a place in which you want to remain. You were meant to be healed. God designed your body that way.

Initially, the covering of the wound is important to the healing process. The formation of the scab is just as important. There are several purposes for the scab. The presence of the scab is part of the healing process as well. Actually, this is one of the signs that your body is healing itself. It is so amazing how God actually formed our physical body to heal itself (Kudos for God!). The scab is a protective cap over the wound that helps to prevent dirt and germs from entering the wound. It also helps to limit your level of blood loss, guard the wound against infection and stabilizes the wound. Plus, while the scab is forming, underneath the scab new skins cells are being formed. The scab remains firmly in place until this process is complete.

I liken the scab that forms on the wound to God's way of covering and comforting us in the midst of the tough times in our lives. In the midst of our hurtful experiences, God will give us just what we need to comfort, protect and strengthen us again. Underneath the disappointments, hurt and abuse is a pearl waiting to be resurfaced. Yes, you are coming out of that rubble! Allow God to heal you from the inside out so you can become a better you.

Becoming better and experiencing the best in our relationships is something we all want to attain, but there are times when we find ourselves on a continual cycle of being hurt. After you've been hurt several times in different relationships, you might begin to ask, "Why is this happening to me?" or "Why does this keep happening to me?" For some reason you keep meeting the same kind of men who keep hurting you.

➢ Has your self-esteem level dropped so low that you've settled for mistreatment in a relationship? Why are you accepting this?

_____

_____

_____

_____

_____

➢ Have you begun to recognize that you are beginning to compromise your standards just to be in the arms of a man? Be honest. If so, what are the signs that made you recognize this?

_____

_____

_____

_____

Questions like these will help you to determine whether these kinds of hurtful relationships are happening because of you, him or both of you.

Unfortunately, some of the wounds we suffered from were created by us. I know you're saying, "You've got to be kidding me? Why would I bring this on myself?" Hear me out. No one really likes to admit that they are the reason for their hurt, but in some cases we really are to blame. This is because many of us have allowed individuals in our lives that didn't know how to handle our heart. We allowed these people to mistreat us even though we knew deep within ourselves that we deserved better. The red flag, the stop sign and all the warning signals were all there in the beginning to prompt us to walk away from the very relationship that in the end seemed to hurt us the most. We gave them an inch and they took the whole field! Sometimes we tolerated the mistreatment just so we would have someone in our lives. Open your eyes and stop falling for that foolishness. The package may look good to the eyes, but the contents are definitely unacceptable.

Then again, it might be him. Sometimes the wounds are formed because someone else is to blame. You did everything right, the connection was there and the relationship seemed to be going so well and then it happens. He drops you—with no explanation and no warning as if you were just another woman to add to his player list. Out of the blue, he starts putting you down, humiliating you in public and then he hits you that very first time. What you are experiencing is the real 'him' beginning to surface beyond his display of kind character. I'm sure he kept his swinish ways hidden for as long as he could. It was inevitable that in a matter of time he would take off his sheep clothing and expose his swinish character (Remember we're talking about swinish men only because a good man will always know how to love and respect a lady).

> From your experience, was it you or him that created the wounds you suffered? How could you have handled it differently?

_____

_____

_____

_____

_____

_____

Unfortunately when you get involved with a swinish man he usually doesn't care about you or anything that has to do with you. He really doesn't understand how to care for, much less how to treat a woman. He likes to play mind games and he will belittle anything about you. He wants control. In his eyes he thinks he's Mr. Right, but little does he know his stuff is stinking louder than a pile of pig's slop. He's in the pig pen snorting at your very presence hoping you'll be fool enough to come in to eat his slop. Abusive men and men with unhealthy characteristics need help, and usually, the people they get involved with aren't the ones who help them. Stay away from swinish men (abusers: physical, verbal, spiritual, sexual and emotional) because the end results of these kinds of relationships could cost you your life—literally.

Sometimes both of you need inner healing. When two wounded people get involved in a relationship together, one of two things will happen; either the two of you will continue to hurt each other, or someone will get enough courage to leave the relationship. Leaving the relationship is what you need to strongly consider. Holding onto someone who continually hurts you is foolish. You should love yourself better than that. Believe me; you won't be lonely without him. Rather, you'll be at peace. Walk away and take time to heal.

> ➤ Are you in a relationship now that you think you should walk away from? What are some of the signs to indicate that?

_____

_____

_____

_____

_____

_____

When we don't take the time to heal from our hurt, usually the hurt begins to grow and take other forms. It will affect any relationship you are connected to. Before you know it, you're going off on people at the drop of a hat. This is because hurt people, hurt other people. When you are filled with frustration and bitterness, you're not easy to forgive and have not healed from the hurts in your past; you will hurt others until you completely heal. We see this cycle occurring when abused people abuse others. Even though the abused person hated the abuse while it was happening to them, ironically the abused later becomes the abuser.

If you don't take the time to heal, you will find yourself trying to fill a void in your life with any man who comes along. I don't know how it's possible, but somehow our hurt attracts others who hurt. If a woman comes out of an abusive relationship, she must be very careful when she gets involved in her next relationship. She must make sure she takes the time to heal; otherwise, she may find herself in the same kind of relationship. At first she may not notice it, but as she continues in the relationship she may later realize that the same characteristics of the person who hurt her in the first place are now in the new person she's currently involved herself with.

Sometimes we find ourselves in a different relationship only to later realize that the same characteristics of the old relationship are in the new.

➢ Have you found that same cycle in the relationships that you've connected with? If so, why do you think that is happening?

_____

_____

_____

_____

_____

_____

➤ Are you in a relationship that has the same characteristics as your last relationship? If so what are they?

_____

_____

_____

_____

The hurt, if not dealt with, will follow you into the next relationship whether you intended it to or not. Some people call it, "old baggage." You can't bring it into a relationship and expect the relationship to last. When we carry "old baggage" into a new relationship, the new man involved with you tends to suffer because of the emotional damage that the former companion inflicted on you. If he's a good man, that's not fair to him because he didn't hurt you. He only wants to love you. It's good to have your guard up, but don't make him suffer for what someone else did to you.

The Bible shares with us how new wine shouldn't be poured into old skins (Matthew 9:17) because the bottles will break. You can't expect to be treated as delicately as a pearl by jumping from one relationship to the next without first being healed. A new relationship never heals the old wounds. It's a temporary fix. Ask the woman at the well (John 4). I'm sure she can give you an earful about jumping in and out of relationships and how her thirst was never quenched. (It wasn't until she met the best man ever...His name was Jesus!) Getting a new man in your life is not what healing is all about. He really isn't your source of healing; he's just another form of cover-up.

➤ Have you been guilty of jumping in and out of relationships to heal your pain? How did that make you feel?

_____

_____

_____

_____

Covering up your hurt never completes the healing; it only soothes you temporarily. Have you ever had one of those closets or one of those rooms that no one is allowed to go in? It's a room or closet filled with so much junk that if anyone tried to come in they would be bombarded with clothing, old books, old pictures, old toys, and a whole bunch of other stuff nobody uses anymore or refuses to throw away. Yet, all that stuff stays in there until someone has the courage to clean it up. This is how we do when we've been wounded. We throw it all in a room; shut the door and walk away thinking the stuff is going to go away. Many of us believe that if we don't deal with it, it will go away. This is not always the case when it comes to becoming emotionally healed. Sooner or later we will have to address it. Not dealing with it doesn't make it go away; nor does it heal us. Many of us have done such a good job with packing it down, sweeping it under the rug and putting on our mask to display our strength, but inwardly we are suffering in silence. I call it the cover-up phases in our lives.

The cover-up phase comes in different forms. Some women have resorted to drugs, alcohol, sex, and working extensively to ease the pain of their hurt. They use things and people to camouflage the hurt they've managed to keep packed down for a long time. Women who use these methods will never experience true healing.

Some women resort to connecting with God as a means to heal their wounds. Of course, running to God for comfort is ideal, scriptural and highly recommended. Yet, there are many women in church who are hurting and are still trying to portray that they have everything together. They are more concerned about what other people will say or how other people will perceive them as a Christian woman. They will jump around the church and shout when the praises go up, they will speak in other tongues, shake and even quote scriptures verbatim and still be hurting. I'm not downing the church or God. I'm writing this because I know. I've been there. Yes, you can be saved, sanctified and filled with the Holy Ghost, but still hurt. Suffering in silence because you don't want anyone to know what you're dealing with because it might portray to others that you are a weak Christian.

> Is this you? Have you covered your hurt so others won't see? Is it helping you to do this?

_____

_____

_____

_____

_____

_____

Sister, it's time to take the mask off and allow God to begin the healing process in your heart. The enemy wants you to suffer in silence. He wants you to keep that hurt and bitterness in your heart so you won't ever love or be loved again, but the devil is a liar! The Church is a place of healing. Change takes place when we enter into the house of worship and hear God's Word. If you have to cry out in the service, roll on the floor, run to the altar for prayer; do it. Don't worry about what others will think or what they will say. You need to be whole. Focus on that. If you need counseling, get it. The scriptures tell us that in the multitude of counselors there is safety. Allow the healing process to begin. Talk to God. Talk with someone.

There are times even after we've experienced wholeness when the scars are still there. Even though the scars from the old hurt may still be there, you don't need to continue to be hurt by it. Have you ever looked at your body and noticed the scars still on your body? Isn't it funny how some scars heal totally, some fade away and others still remain on our bodies? Scars are reminders of what happened and of what God brought us through. Even though the scar is still there, you know that you've been healed.

Knowing that you've been healed is your breakthrough moment. Yes, the scar is there and yes, the situation did happen in your life, but it doesn't have to hurt anymore. That's exactly where God wants you to be…where it doesn't hurt anymore. Reach out to God and allow Him to get you to that point. Let Him put you on the potter's wheel and make you over again (Jeremiah 18). Momma did a good job in comforting you when you fell down, but God knows exactly how to comfort you far beyond momma's touch.

Chapter 5 – Blast from the Past

<u>SHAME</u>

"That's a shame." "You ought to be ashamed of yourself." "Shame on you." "Have you no shame?" These sayings may be something you've heard people say or either you said them yourself. The word 'shame' is defined as being, *"a feeling of guilt, regret, or sadness that you have because you know you have done something wrong."*

Shame. The word shame is something that I recently realized had been hanging around me for years. I couldn't understand why I acted a certain way, didn't fully show up and was still hesitant about talking about certain things that took place in my past. I started to see how this word; shame was affecting my life in many ways. The feelings of shame were planted in me in my childhood. The emotions that were attached to the feelings of shame were never really addressed so the residue of it would resurface every now and then. After all these years, I thought I had done a great job of keeping those feelings of shame packed down and hidden. The emotions that went along with the shame and embarrassment I felt really didn't come alive again until something I did or something someone said about my faults. As those feelings emerged, it would cause me to crawl in a ball, not physically, but inwardly I would close up and go in hiding because of it. I'd shut myself off from others if I had to in order to protect my heart from the pain of shame.

I'm sure we all can say that there are some things that have taken place in our lives that we are ashamed of and we wished had never occurred. And, if we could do it all over again, we would do things differently without question.

However, those things did happen and those things were said. You and I can't change it even if we tried. The only thing we can do now is not allow those things that happened to cause us to continue to walk in the spirit of shame. The spirit of shame will cause you to go in hiding. This place called, "hiding" is where people go when they are experiencing shame because of what took place in their past. In hiding, you don't give yourself the liberty to walk in your purpose, go after your dreams and many have difficulty connecting with the right relationships. The spirit of shame has a root cause. It is a spinoff of fear. You hide because you are in fear of failing, making a mistake or being addressed in front of people that recognize your flaws. Listen, hiding does not resolve the issue. Hiding does not allow you to receive the healing from the shame. Taking the time to address what happened; forgiving yourself and others is the start to healing from the shame.

➢ Have you ever felt ashamed about something? If so, how have you handled it?

_____

_____

_____

➢ What were the emotions you felt because of shame?

_____

_____

_____

➢ Have you gone into hiding because of something you are ashamed of? Share your thoughts about it here.

_____

_____

_____

_____

Another thing that shame will cause you to do is cover up the past so you won't have to confront it or deal with it. The purpose of the cover up is so you don't have to deal with the pain that is associated with the spirit of shame. You feel as though as long as you don't have to confront it, you won't have to experience the pain that it created in the first place. So, you go into denial mode.

Many of us don't want to deal with the baggage that we created. It's too heavy. It's too complicated. It's just too much to deal with, but unless you deal with it, it will always be with you. It will follow you in your next relationship, in your marriage, on your job, in your business, in your ministry and even in your children if you don't catch it. Listen, face the music; you made a mistake, but that doesn't mean you are a mistake. The first order of business is to forgive yourself. You must dig deep, uproot that pain of the shame and allow yourself to heal. Sometimes digging deep may require for you to go to counseling and that's okay. Going to counseling is not a sign of weakness, but on the contrary a sign of strength. It shows that you care enough about yourself to get the help you need...period. Don't be ashamed to get the help. Covering up the pain from our past never heals it; it only soothes it temporarily. Temporary fixes, eventually, will backfire on you.

➢ Have you tried to cover up or mask the shame? If so, how?

_____

_____

_____

_____

_____

_____

➢ Have you ever attended counseling? If so, how was your experience?

_____

_____

_____

_____

_____

_____

Listen, if you don't allow yourself to heal, shame will cause you to cover up so much, that you will begin to move away from authenticity and gravitate towards becoming fake. Yes, I said it. You become a fake person; a person who you have created so that you don't have to deal with the shame. You wear the mask to cover up what you really don't want revealed. People pack down their reality, cover it up and even move into denial just because they don't want to deal with the shame. People do this because they are ashamed of who they are or what they have done.

Sometimes you find this in marital relationships. When a woman is in a relationship that is unhealthy, she may deny anything that indicates that she is in an abusive relationship because she is ashamed of it. The shame comes because she knows that if people really knew how she lived, it would blow their mind. She's made every attempt to make people believe the fake story and her fake identity so she doesn't have to address it. Therefore, to cover it up, she goes in hiding because of the shame she feels. Fear is the root of it. Putting on the mask and living a non-authentic life will get tiresome. You have to come to grips with what is really happening and be true to yourself. Be honest where you are right now. Be honest with yourself because that is only when God or anyone else can really give you the help you need to overcome this spirit of shame. William Shakespeare said it perfectly, "To thine own self be true." We have all made mistakes, but don't allow those mistakes to block the full potential of your destiny.

➢ Name something mentioned above that really stood out to you.

_____

_____

_____

_____

_____

This is a scripture that has blessed me so much when it came to dealing with shame. *Isaiah 61:7 "For your shame ye shall have double; and for confusion they shall rejoice in their portion: therefore in their land they shall possess the double: everlasting joy shall be unto them."* The reason this scripture blessed me is because it told me that I was going to get double for my shame. We often hear people say, "Double for my trouble." Well, that's exactly how I looked at it. There is double (blessings) coming your way because of the shame you experienced. Rest in that. Let your mind be at peace because of that. You can't allow yourself to get stuck in your feelings of shame because that will only stagnate your progress in life. It is a process that requires you to let it go and release it from your heart. You can't change what you experienced, but you can learn from it. Keeping the feelings of shame bottled up inside of you will interfere with your process of loving who you are. Forgive yourself, let it go, heal and move on.

> ➤ What are some of the things you will do to help you let go of those feelings of shame?

_____

_____

_____

_____

> ➤ What are your feelings about the scripture, Isaiah 6:7?

_____

_____

_____

_____

Sometimes talking about the incidents with trustworthy people will assist you in getting through the feelings of shame. There are some people that actually share their experiences with others for the purpose of helping someone else get through. You see, you have to get through this, because then you can turn around and help someone else get through it.

> ➢ If you had to share your experience about your feelings of shame with someone else, what would it be?

_____

_____

_____

_____

_____

_____

GUILT

Dealing with guilt can eat at you from your core. Guilt and shame sometimes go hand and hand. Usually you feel guilty about what you did and you experience the feelings of shame because of it. The word guilt is defined as being, *"a bad feeling caused by knowing or thinking that you have done something bad or wrong."* The key to healing from the feelings of guilt is to be honest with yourself about it. If you know you did something inappropriate, don't lie about it or deny it; at least not to yourself. Face it head on and allow the healing process to begin.

There are a few things to consider assisting you in moving beyond the guilt:

> Watch your self-talk. Don't waste your entire life trying to beat yourself up about what happened. You can't change it.
> Don't focus on the negative feedback because of it. Forgive yourself, learn from it and move on.
> Don't allow others to keep reminding you of what happened; even after many years later. Kindly let them know that you regret what happened, but you are moving on from that point.
> Evaluate what you've learned. What did you learn? What would you have changed about your choices? What would you tell others to warn them about it? Reflect on this and write down some points.

_____

_____

_____

_____

_____

> Move forward, love who you are and dream again. What will you do with your life now? What will you do differently?

_____

_____

_____

_____

The interesting thing about the Apostle Paul in the Bible is that he spent many years of persecuting the church. He even had the audacity to encourage that Christians be killed because they believed on the message of Jesus Christ. However, after his encounter with Jesus Christ, his life changed and he didn't get stuck in the emotional feelings of guilt. This is what he says in scripture (Philippians 3:13), *"Brethren, I count not myself to have apprehended: but this one thing I do, forgetting those things which are behind, and reaching forth unto those things which are before,"*

The Apostle Paul recognized the importance of forgetting those things which were behind him; the guilt, the mistakes and the criticism of others. He must have realized that looking back was going to prohibit him from reaching forward to the great things God had in store for his life. This is the same for you. There are so many great things in store for your life, but the way you get to them is pushing beyond your guilty feelings. You can't change yesterday, but you can make the right choices going forward for your todays and your tomorrows. You have the ability to get through this and you will.

➢ What does the scripture in Philippians 3:13 mean to you? Reflect on it.

_____

_____

_____

_____

_____

PAST MISTAKES

The mistakes made are simply a blast from the past. Somehow, no matter what you do, something from your past will resurface. And it seems as though it resurfaces at the strangest times. When you have decided to move forward and things are really beginning to make a turn for you, the past mistakes resurface. They resurface many times through your thoughts and through other individuals that remember your mistakes.

Sometimes your thoughts will play a mean trick on you and play back a scenario that took place in your life that involved your past mistakes. This can cause you to experience the same emotions that took place way back when the mistakes took place. The purpose of the playback is to cause you to become stagnate, stuck on the feelings of guilt and shame that you may have felt because of the past mistakes. When that playback occurs, you really have to make every effort to redirect your thoughts towards something more positive about who you are. Your mistakes are not the totality of who you are as an individual so don't let the past mistakes dictate your destiny.

> ➢ Are there some things from your past that resurface in your thoughts at certain times? If so, what are they?

_____

_____

_____

_____

➢ How do you handle those negative thoughts of your past?

_____

_____

_____

_____

I know there are some things you may not be proud of. Listen, we all have skeletons in the closet that we wish never existed. There are things all of us wish we had never done, said or entertained, but it happened. I'm going to repeat something that I know many people have said to you before, "Let it go! Forgive yourself and move on." You really have to do just that....let it go. Holding onto it only holds you hostage. It will only keep you stuck in time. Your body will continue to grow and develop, but your mind is stuck in the past when you made the mistake. Release yourself from that bondage. No matter what others are saying; don't allow their words to hold you hostage and don't you allow yourself to do it either. Tell yourself, "I am forgiven."

➢ Are you willing to forgive yourself concerning your past? Repeat these phrases and write them down: "I'm going to let the pain of my past go. I forgive myself and I'm going to move on. I am forgiven."

_____

_____

_____

_____

➢ How did it feel to actually say those phrases aloud? What were some of the emotions that you experienced while saying them?

_____

_____

_____

_____

_____

You can't change the past, but you can change how you react to it when it's brought up by others.

You can't change the past even if you really tried. What you can do is change how you react to what is discussed about your past and the thoughts that come to your mind. When your past is discussed you can calmly and firmly remind the person that this is not who you are right now and that you have grown since that mistake. Technically, you really don't owe them an explanation about what happened in the past, but if you desire to share, remain calm about it. No need to get yourself in a ruckus about something that happened so long ago or that you can't change.

When the thoughts come in your mind to plague you with feelings of guilt and shame about your past, you must be willing to shift your mind on purpose. You may have to say aloud, "I did it. I forgive myself and that is not who I am now."

You see, you determine how you'll handle the blast from the past when it comes your way. You don't have to defend yourself, explain yourself or clear yourself unless you choose to do so. I can't emphasize enough that you can't change it, but you can do something about your overall behavior going forward. Forgive yourself, forgive others involved and move on because greatness awaits you. You are overdue in loving who you are. Your journey towards wholeness and loving you begins with forgiving and letting go of those things that have taken place from your past.

> What were some of the points that really stood out to you in the paragraphs in this section?

_____

_____

_____

_____

_____

_____

> How will these points change your thinking about you and your past?

_____

_____

_____

_____

_____

_____

UNDERESTIMATED

Another person's opinion of your capabilities doesn't determine what you can or cannot do. Just because a person doesn't think you are capable of doing something or becoming something doesn't mean you can't. They just don't know all that is within you. They have already prejudged what you can do based on their perception of you, but your abilities are not limited to their way of thinking.

> ➢ Have you ever felt underestimated by others? If so, how did it make you feel?

_____

_____

_____

_____

When a person sees your abilities displayed openly, they are initially shocked because in their mind, they underestimated you. They didn't realize all that was in you. You have to really be careful about connecting with individuals that underestimate you because they will always keep you at a level that is below your capabilities. If they have never seen what you can do, they are only left to assume that you can only do what you've shown them. However, different surroundings, different people and different circumstances sometimes have a way of bringing more out of us. When it appears as though that you are not birthing out the best of you, sometimes it is because your surroundings are stagnating you. Sometimes those surroundings include individuals within your inner circle that suffocate your ability to grow, develop and thrive. Love yourself enough to recognize when to disconnect from some connections.

> Have you ever been held back on utilizing your gifts and talents because you knew the people around you didn't believe in you? What were your feelings? What was your response to it?

_____

_____

_____

_____

_____

_____

Sometimes the reason we walk in our fullest potential is because we recognize who we are. When you begin to believe in yourself and see that your life is destined for greatness, you will walk in dignity and pride. This may cause others to be shocked because they quite possibly could have underestimated you. They didn't realize that you had all of that in you. You see, when you truly love who you are, you're not concerned about the opinions of others anyway. Walk in your fullest potential today. Don't shortchange or settle anymore. Stretch yourself. Sometimes when you stretch yourself, you may even be shocked what you can do. This only happens if you have underestimated yourself. You need to begin to recognize, acknowledge and act upon all that God has given you. Love the person He has created you to be. If you begin to underestimate yourself in your own abilities, then so will others. You better recognize what who you are and what you are capable of. Greatness is within you.

> Have you ever underestimated yourself? If so why?

_____

_____

_____

_____

You are not inferior to anyone. You have so much to bring to the table. If people can't recognize your value, then don't waste your time trying to convince them. You don't have to beg anybody to be with you, to work with you nor do you have to beg to work with anyone else. Recognize your capabilities, your strengths, your talents, your anointing and operate in it fluently. Your abilities were given to you for a divine purpose. Don't allow anyone else to cause you to think less of yourself. Don't be moved by other people's opinion of you. If they underestimate who you are and don't tap into what you bring to the table, then they will just miss out.

OVERLOOKED

Have you ever been in a room or in a particular organization or church and everyone notices and/or acknowledges other people, but they overlook you totally? You may have answered yes to this, but let me assure you that your life is significant and what you bring to the table matters.

Sometimes you may have wondered if they noticed that you existed. Sometimes that little small voice within you may even be screaming out to them...."I'm right here."

Sometimes you may be overlooked when it comes to not being considered for a particular job or position. You know you have the skill and/or expertise, but for some reason you are overlooked. The feeling of being overlooked has happened to me on several occasions. At the time, it hurt because I wondered why they overlooked me when I felt I was qualified. Sometimes you feel qualified or you actually are qualified to fulfill the assignment, but for some reason the person, needing the assistance doesn't see it that way at the time.

There may be a relationship that you are currently involved in and the person you are connected to may overlook you at times. I know you can agree that no one likes to be overlooked by the one they love. Love yourself enough to have a conversation with that person and express your feelings.

I learned some things from being overlooked: 1) You really may not be qualified in that timing/season or for that position. There could possibly be an area in your life that you need to perfect or get better at in order to walk in those shoes. This doesn't mean that you are not good enough, but it just could possibly mean that you are not ready for that area just yet.

2) The person and/or individuals have their own insecurities and if they acknowledge you or you are selected for something renowned, it will make them look bad. They are in fear that people will take notice of you more than they would take notice of them.

3) Sometimes being overlooked is God's way of protecting you. Sometimes God hides you on purpose. Overlooked by man, but recognized by God. Sometimes there are

individuals and places that God does not want you to be associated with so He will intentionally cause those individuals to overlook you. It may not feel good initially, but the outcome of it all is far greater than the feelings you may have because of it.

It's similar to why some children don't fit in with certain peer groups. They may want to fit in with the popular crowd, but somehow they don't. It could very well be that God is shielding and protecting them from something that would do them harm down the road. You may be overlooked by man, but God recognizes exactly who you are. His plan far exceeds the people or group of people that may not see your greatness at first sight.

> Have you ever been overlooked? If so, how did it make you feel?

_____

_____

_____

_____

> If you've been overlooked, how did you handle it then? How would you handle it now?

_____

_____

_____

_____

MISUNDERSTOOD

You may be thinking, I didn't mean to say it like that, do it like that or for it to be interpreted in that way. They said you said or did it that way, but you tried to explain to them that you didn't mean it to appear that way. The more you tried to explain yourself, the more they looked at you as though your words were meaningless. I hate to tell you, but you've been misunderstood.

Being misunderstood is not a good feeling when it initially happens. You know what you felt in your heart to do and what you meant to say, but because of the interpretation of another; it was taken out of context.

> ➤ Have you ever been misunderstood? If so, share your experience.

_____

_____

_____

_____

> ➤ Have you ever misunderstood someone else's actions? What did they do to cause you to misunderstand them?

_____

_____

_____

_____

Sometimes when people misunderstand you it is based on their own way of thinking. Their perception of what you are doing or saying is usually mixed in with their mindset and belief system. They may misunderstand because they see it a different way. Sometimes the person you have a misunderstanding with has other individuals in their lives filling them with their point of view, which can create an even greater misunderstanding. This is why so many people part in relationships because of misunderstandings. One person did or said something and the other person misinterpreted the other person's action the wrong way. Sometimes, in many instances, a simple conversation can break the yoke that has wrapped around the individuals.

A simple conversation with those who misunderstood you could change things for the better.

> ➤ Who are the individuals or person that you need to have a conversation with to clear up a misunderstanding? What will you say?

_____

_____

_____

_____

_____

_____

Some people may not hear your explanation because they are set on what they believe. You can't change it no matter how hard you try to explain. Share your heart and then move on. Know that you did your best. Rest in that.

REJECTION

Rejection is difficult to accept when it is initially displayed. No one wants to be rejected, but it has happened to us all at some point in our lives. You may remember a time when that boy you were so interested in really wasn't interested in you. At that time, you probably wondered why he didn't like you. What was wrong with you? You began to examine yourself trying to figure out reasons why he didn't want to be with you. Some of those feelings of rejection hurt deep and some you managed to brush them off. Oftentimes, we question what is wrong with us instead of coming to the conclusion that quite possibly the person just wasn't a good fit for us. There is nothing wrong with you. Love you are.

Some of us have dealt with that same feeling in our adulthood. There may be certain groups that you didn't connect with for whatever reason. You may never know why they really rejected you from their groups. Don't concern yourself with that. There is a reason for all things. I know that rejection hurt you initially. However, if you take a moment to look back at some of those scenarios of being rejected from specific individuals or groups, you may find that it was a blessing in disguise.

> ➢ Who has rejected you in your life? How did that experience make you feel?

_____

_____

_____

_____

➢ How did you handle and/or cope with the rejection that you received?

_____

_____

_____

_____

_____

➢ What were some of the results of how you handled rejection in the past?

_____

_____

_____

_____

_____

➢ What would you do differently now when it comes to confronting rejection?

_____

_____

_____

_____

_____

_____

Chapter 6: Forgiveness

Let's face it, sometimes our past experiences and past failures make us feel as though we are not good enough. Some of us may even feel that we are a complete failure. So we walk around with this weight on our shoulders thinking because of what we did or didn't do; makes us unworthy. We walked around as if there is no opportunity for reconciliation or forgiveness.

My dear Sister, you must forgive yourself for what happened. You can only make decisions based on what you know and what you believe to be true. At that time, you acted upon what you knew then. You can't beat yourself up for not knowing how you could have properly handled that situation. You also can't continue to beat yourself up for making a choice that you knew could possibly have affected you and others in a negative way. Breathe. It's over, so give yourself a break from what happened. You can't change it anyway. Forgive yourself, forgive others, learn from the experience and move on.

You may have heard someone say that we are our worst critic. At times, I really think there is some truth to it especially when we've done something that we are ashamed of or have failed at something. After the experience we tend to beat ourselves up by constantly reminding ourselves of our mistake. We do this through our thoughts and the words we say. The enemy does a great job of reminding us of what we did wrong. He will constantly taunt us by using individuals to rehearse our failures in our ears. Instead of forgiving ourselves and letting go of what happened, we get stuck in the past. Not being able to let go and forgive yourself will only hold you hostage.

You can't change the past or change what happened. However, you can change how you will respond to the negative thoughts or words spoken about your past. It all starts with forgiving yourself. There is no need to put yourself down any further. It's time to move on with your life. Stop beating yourself up about it; move on with your life. There are so many great things in store for your future, but in order to fully enjoy them you have to forgive yourself.

> What has happened in your life that you have not forgiven yourself for?

_____

_____

_____

_____

I'm sure there have been times where you have been done wrong by another. It happens to us all. Not everyone is going to do right by you, but that doesn't mean it's a good thing to hold grudges against them. Holding the grudge never really works out for the person who does. Holding onto the old pain that you experienced from them doesn't free you. It keeps you bound and they move on with their lives. Your responsibility is to forgive so it frees you up to receive the continual pouring of blessings over your life.

> Is there anyone that you feel as though you haven't forgiven?

_____

_____

_____

> Why are you holding it?

_____

_____

_____

_____

> Is it really making a difference for you by holding onto it?

_____

_____

_____

I must encourage you to do something. It may be difficult at first, but I believe you can do it. Say aloud, "I forgive myself. I release myself from the pain, guilt and shame. I forgive myself." Then forgive the person or individuals that have done you wrong. "I forgive _____ for _____. I forgive them now and I choose to walk in love."

Congratulations, you are on the road to beginning the healing process through forgiveness. Yes, it is a process and time will heal the wound as you allow yourself to walk in forgiveness. As you forgive others, please remember to forgive yourself. It's a daily commitment, but you can do this. Doing so signifies that you love yourself enough to forgive you. Moving on and pressing on beyond it will cause you to experience a greater level of living. You can't change what happened, but you can change how you react to it. Free yourself through forgiveness.

Chapter 7: Words You Say & Hear

During the course of your lifetime, there may have been people that have said things that may have hurt you. At times, I'm sure those words resonate in your heart. They may even bring on the same emotion that they did when you first heard it. However, the way to combat that is to have your own voice. You must speak up for you. You can begin to speak positively over those words that caused you pain. Your words carry just as much weight as the other person, if not more. You have the final say so of the outcome of the words spoken by others. What they said doesn't have to happen or have a negative effect on you anymore. You have power through your own voice. It doesn't matter what they've said. That's done and over with.....finished. What matters is what you are speaking over your life right now. The past is something you cannot change, but you have the ability, authority and power to speak into your life and into your future by your own words.

You see, words create so much. It was God that gave us this ability. He spoke and it came to pass. Your words have that impact, especially over your own life. So don't allow the negative words of others from the past to continue to move you. Speak back to it!

When King David went to battle against Goliath, he didn't allow the words of his accuser to paralyze him. Instead, David used his own words and spoke back. He was not about to allow Goliath to have the final say concerning his life or the outcome of Israel's victory. You too, must use your words to speak over your life in a positive way.

Words have a direct impact on our behaviors, our moods and our actions.

Many times, we may not realize the effects of our own words. I found this out the hard way at one point in my life. I can remember complaining about a situation to the point that anytime a person would give a listening ear, I would complain about it. It was so heavy on me that I felt that it was best to talk about it just so I could get if off my chest. I soon found out that my negative spoken words were actually creating what I complained about. Instead of the situation getting better, it got worse. Part of that, I believe, had a lot to do with my words that I was speaking out of my own mouth.

> ➤ What are some of the things that you are saying about your situation or circumstance? Are you seeing what you said?

_____

_____

_____

_____

> ➤ What are some of the things that you have been saying about yourself?

_____

_____

_____

_____

➤ If those words are negative, write the opposite of what you are saying and create a positive phrase.

_____

_____

_____

_____

Whether you realize it or not, your words have the ability to create what you desire for your life. You can begin to call those things that be not as though they were (Romans 4:17). Speak what you desire to take place in your life by saying what you really want to happen in your life. Don't allow yourself to be moved by what you see with a natural eye, as I did, but speak into the atmosphere beyond what you see until you see it. Yes, say it until you see it.

➤ Take a moment and write down some of the things you really want to take place in your life. Then, begin to say it out of your own mouth on a daily basis.

_____

_____

_____

_____

_____

When you think about something and then speak it out, you give what you said permission to be activated in your life. I remember hearing my mother tell me, "Think before you speak." At that time, she wanted me to be mindful of what I spoke because what I said could affect everything around me. Your words are powerful. So choose your words wisely as you speak out what you really want for your life.

Words spoken out of your mouth are a direct reflection on what is in your heart. Sometimes we have to take a moment to take inventory on what is coming out of our mouths. If you are filled with frustration, anxiety and/or have feelings of low self-esteem, your words will reflect that because this is what is within your heart.

The whole concept of loving who you are from the inside out must begin from within. The love that you have or don't have within for yourself will come out. If your words are not in alignment with valuing and loving who you are, then it's time to check your inner feelings and thoughts.

➤ Monitor your words for the next seven days and write down the positive and negative words/statements that you are saying.

_____

_____

_____

_____

_____

_____

_____

➢ What kind of pattern do you see with the words you
   are speaking?

_____

_____

_____

_____

_____

_____

_____

Take the time to review what you have been saying on a
daily basis.   What you have been saying has already
manifested in your life right now. So if you don't like what
you see, change what you're saying.

What you're saying is also a direct result of what you are
feeling from within.   Your words are expressions of the
emotions you have from within. Loving who you are begins
from the inside out. Allow the inner woman (you) to heal so
that you can begin to actually speak what you want and not
what you fear.

Say what you really want for your life until you see it.

Words We Hear

As you may already know, words impact us in many ways. The words that we heard when we were young girls have followed many of us well into our adulthood. Sometimes those words were positive and reassuring and then there were times when they were negative and degrading. Some of the words playback in our ears and most of the times the words still create the same effect now as they did when they were first spoken. As the Bible declares that, "Death and Life are in the power of the tongue…" ~ Proverbs 18:21.

Let's address the negative and degrading talk that has been voiced in your presence. These kinds of conversations could have happened in your childhood with a parent or family member. It could have happened in your adulthood while dealing with some of your friends, boyfriends and/or spouse.

> ➢ What were some of the negative words you heard about you coming up as a child?

_____

_____

_____

_____

_____

_____

_____

➢ Do you remember how you felt when you first heard those words? Share your feelings here. When was it exactly?

_____

_____

_____

_____

_____

_____

➢ How do those words affect you today?

_____

_____

_____

_____

➢ What are some of the negative words that have been said to you recently in life?

_____

_____

_____

_____

➤ What has been your reaction to those words?

_____

_____

_____

_____

_____

➤ What do you think you can do differently now in handling negative words spoken to you?

_____

_____

_____

_____

_____

The key to handling negative spoken words in your life is to not allow them to settle into your heart (your spirit). You don't want them to take root and grow there because then other emotions begin to surface in your life. These emotions could be bitterness, hatred, jealousy, rejection and un-forgiveness to name a few. These emotions create behaviors that would not exemplify a woman who knows her worth, recognizes her value or even loves who she is. You might even ask how I can keep these negative words from controlling my thinking or behavior. You have to catch those negative words when they surface in your mind and eradicate them by replacing them with positive words. Oftentimes, this is done through speaking God's Word over your life, speaking positively into your own life and by connecting with those who will speak positive words of affirmation to you.

Words generate thoughts and thoughts turn into action if carried out. When negative words are spoken into our lives they filter into our thought life. You have to be diligent about capturing those negative words. The concept of capturing those negative words and eradicating them all begins with applying God's Word. In Second Corinthians 10:5 it shares this, *"Casting down imaginations, and every high thing that exalteth itself against the knowledge of God, and bringing into captivity every thought to the obedience of Christ;....."* We must take the initiative in capturing the thoughts that mean us harm and bring them into obedience to God's Word. If the words spoken towards you don't line up with God's Word concerning who you are, then don't let them become a part of your daily thoughts.

Not only must you be mindful of whom you allow to speak into your life, but you must also monitor what you are saying about yourself. This begins in our thoughts, but when our thoughts are expressed they turn into words. Our own personal words that we say about ourselves and our situations can be very influential in what outcomes we experience. The Bible tells us in Proverbs 6:2, *"Though art snared with the words of thy mouth, thou art taken with the words of thy mouth."* Our words get us in situations that can be beneficial or very harmful. We talk ourselves into things and we also talk ourselves out of things. We snare ourselves with our own words when we talk ourselves out of pursuing our dreams, going after a promotion, walking in our divine purpose, walking in wealth and so much more. Sometimes we allow fear to dictate our words. We speak what we see instead of what we want to take place in our lives. You have to call those things that be not as though they were (Romans 4:17). You have to be mindful of what you are calling to yourself through the words that you speak out of your mouth.

➤ What are some of the things that you have talked yourself out of because of fear?

_____

_____

_____

_____

➤ What results are you getting based on the words you are saying out of your own mouth?

_____

_____

_____

➤ Based on the answer above, do you feel you need to change what you say?

_____

_____

_____

_____

_____

I mentioned this previously, but I want to mention it again here. There was a time in my life when I was going through some things in my life and I can remember that I kept speaking about what was happening over and over and over again. Nothing was changing because all I kept doing was talk about it and talk about it and talk about it again. I began to see the manifestation of what I was complaining about. I wondered why things didn't change. Instead of changing, the struggle began to magnify more. I learned from that experience a few things.

First thing, I learned that I had to be quiet; especially if I wasn't going to speak the right things about my situation. Secondly, I had to learn to call out in the atmosphere (in prayer) what I wanted to happen instead of what I saw happening. Thirdly, I had to reposition myself by focusing on what I personally had to change about me to help my situation. I had to redirect my energy so that I wouldn't get in my emotions, which in turn would cause me to say emotionally driven words instead of what God had to say about it.

I had to speak positive over what didn't appear to look positive until it became positive.

I learned these few things in that season of my life. I'm happy to say that I came through that season and I'm so glad that season is over. Speak positively over your life, your marriage, your children, your finances, your business; your ministry. Speak the Word over all areas of your life.

> What are some points in the paragraph above that stands out to you?

_____

_____

_____

_____

_____

The positive words that you heard from people are what you want to continue to playback in your mind. These people have your best interest at heart. They want to see you make it in life. Yes, some people in your life want to see you make it. They recognize your value and see the potential of your future dreams happening for you. When you get someone (and/or individuals) in your life that is in your corner, hold onto them. Don't let anyone else try to sever the connection of those that affirm you and believe in you. You will need these individuals in your life when you experience the tough times.

It's okay for you to be selective in who pours into you. Not everyone deserves or has the right to speak into your life. The choice of who pastors you (spiritual covering), mentors you, counsels you, coaches and affirms you is important because you give them the authority to influence your life. These kinds of positions should not be taken lightly, but should be filled wisely.

➤ Who are some of the people that speak positively over your life?

_____

_____

_____

_____

_____

_____

➤ What kinds of feelings come when they speak into your life?

_____

_____

_____

_____

➤ What positive things can you say about yourself?

_____

_____

_____

_____

_____

_____

It is essential for you to guard your heart. You are the watchman over your own life. You are the gardener of your own garden. If you see beautiful flowers and greenery in your garden, then that is a direct result of you being attentive to what is being planted in you. If you see a weed patch and dry grass, it is only because the gardener (you) didn't monitor what was being planted. You have to pay close attention to what is being planted in you (words are the seeds) because one day what has been planted will eventually grow. You have the power to determine what grows.

Chapter 8: Appearances

Look at you. No, seriously look at you. Take a moment to look at yourself in the mirror. What do you see? How do you look? What are the first thoughts that come to your mind concerning your outward appearance? Some of you reading this may say that you look good. Some may find fault in what you have on, or how your skin or body looks. Can I let you in on a secret? Always see the good in you. Don't focus so much on the flaws that you see. Some of the flaws you see can be corrected, but some you won't. It's okay…you're still a beautiful lady!

Many times you see women focusing so much on the outward appearance and not taking time to work on the inner woman. This may have been how you felt as well, but I hope after reading through the pages of this book and answering the questions that you've had time to work on the inner woman. Taking the time to empower and beautify yourself inwardly will cause that beautification to exude itself outwardly. Let's face it, you can be beautiful inside and out.

Now please don't get me wrong, inward work is needed, but it's also important for you to be mindful of your outward appearance because this is what people will see first. As we've read in the Bible that man looks on the outward appearance, but God looks at the heart. Man judges by the outward appearance. We all have been guilty of judging a person based on how they looked. We swore up and down we knew their whole life story based on what we perceived about them from the outward appearance only. If we did this ourselves, then you can rest assure that others are doing the same when they see you.

Your outward appearance is the first impression of you. I'm sure you've heard that, "First impressions are lasting impressions." What they see will always remain with them. From this, we can conclude that the outward look and the inward look are both important to maintain. Take pride in how you look. It's okay to do so because it truly reveals that you care about you.

Sometimes when women don't feel good about themselves on the inside, it will reflect outwardly. I know you've seen women who come out of the house with their hair not combed or in a bonnet, rollers in their hair, wearing pajamas on instead of pants, clothes oversized or too tight walking around town. Sometimes we give a poor representation of ourselves because we don't feel that good about who we are inwardly. As women we are known for nurturing and caring for others. It is a part of our nature. At times, we do for others more than we will care for ourselves. Sometimes our focus is not on us at all. We are consumed with taking care of everyone else, that we tend to forget about making sure we look presentable ourselves.

> ➤ Are you guilty of taking care of others before you take care of yourself? In what ways do you do this?

_____

_____

_____

_____

_____

➤ What are some of the reasons why you might neglect your outward appearance?

_____

_____

_____

_____

I'm not saying that you have to be a woman that needs an insurmountable amount of attention or in need of a whole lot of possessions, but you need to have some class about yourself. Feeling good about you will show in all areas of your life. Take care of your skin. Give it the proper treatment to create its beautiful glow. Take care of your hair and do what you can to make it radiant. Wash it, condition it, comb it and brush it. Take care of you. Dress up sometimes. Putting on something nice also helps to make you feel good. Dressing properly and making sure your outward appearance is intact doesn't mean you are selfish, but it does reflect that you care about yourself.

Your outward appearance is a direct reflection of what is taking place inwardly.

The outward is a reflection from the inward. Inwardly we have the ability to shine, which pushes out for all to see. We have to take the time to work from the inside out. This is why it's important to take care of the entire package of YOU. You are important and you matter. Don't allow the inward or the outward to go lacking.

I can't emphasize enough about the importance of healing from the inside out. It's so important to love who you are so that you don't have to entertain the cover-up actions. I know life is not all about your outward appearance, but yet it is important to make sure that your outward appearance is intact. People will judge you by your overall appearance. Yes, I know that shouldn't be your overall concern, but acknowledge the fact that it does exist. Always make a good impression for those you come in contact with.

When you love who you are and value yourself, you will make every effort to make sure to groom your outward appearance properly. Take pride in who you are and how you look. You are a woman of good character and class....walk in that.

Chapter 9: Your Purpose

You have such an amazing life before you. It's filled with meaning and purpose. You see, you're here on purpose for a purpose. There is a significant reason for your existence. God allowed you to be in this season and timeframe to do something great. Yes, you were created to do something great! Let that sink deep in your spirit. The purpose for your life begins from within and you play an essential part in seeing it manifest.

Even though this is true, you've got to believe it. You have to believe that you have a divine purpose and you must be willing to do what is necessary to walk in it. In case you didn't realize this, but loving who you are is so important in regards to you pursuing after your purpose in life. You see, you have to love who you are and believe in yourself in order to move forward in your divine assignment. When you don't fully love yourself, have confidence or believe in yourself, it will cause you to hold back on what you need to accomplish. Not fully loving yourself hinders you from completely yielding to your assignment.

What will happen is you will find yourself taking a few steps, but in the midst of moving forward you won't fully commit to completing the full task. This happens because thoughts of not being worthy and/or lack of self-confidence will begin to pop its head up in your mind. Oftentimes, we self-sabotage our own progress because inwardly we don't love who we are or believe totally in what we want to accomplish. However, recognizing this is the beginning of making the necessary changes to uproot those feelings and that behavior. You have too much to accomplish in this life to allow those feelings and behavior to hinder you any further. Roll up your sleeves and get to work!

> ➢ Are you aware of your purpose and/or divine assignment for your life? Write down your purpose.

_____

_____

_____

_____

_____

> ➢ Do you think that you've played a part in holding back when it comes to walking in your purpose? How?

_____

_____

_____

Name three things that you can do to confront the feelings and/or behavior that comes to hold you back. What will you do differently?

_____

_____

_____

_____

_____

Sometimes we hear people say to get out of your own way. Make sure that the reason you're not walking in your purpose is not solely based on you. Remember you have what it takes to get you to that next step towards your purpose, so go for it.

Having purpose within you is symbolic to a fire ready to spread. Your purpose is waiting to be ignited from within so it can be pushed out into existence. However, if your thoughts and feelings about yourself within are not healthy, then you will be hesitant about moving toward and/or fulfilling your purpose. Loving who you are from the inside out strikes the match to start that fire of purpose to begin its blaze.

What is your passion? What is it that drives you the most? Know what you want and what you want to fulfill in life.

_____

_____

_____

_____

_____

Here are a few things to consider when it comes to purpose.

> Taking the time to understand what your purpose is can be challenging at times, but it's such an essential step to move you towards walking in it and fulfilling it. When you are not fully aware of what your purpose is in life, it will at times cause you to aimlessly walk around being moved by every suggestion for it. Invest the proper time in seeking

God for direction concerning the plan and purpose for your life. God really wants you to know your purpose too. He has plans for your life and He's anticipating for you to walk in its fulfillment. He's counting on you to do this; so go for it.

➢ No matter how hard you may try to push your purpose or divine assignment to the side, it will call you. Yes, purpose is calling you right now. You have something that you must accomplish. Don't underestimate what God has placed inside of you. You have everything you need to accomplish your divine purpose within you. You must believe in you and in the assignment.

➢ Sometimes your purpose will be under attack, but you have to continue to persevere beyond the opposition. Your purpose is far more important than the opposition you may be facing. Encountering opposition while pursuing after your purpose is a clear indication that you are on the right track. The enemy is not going to waste his time to try to block something if it didn't have the capacity to make a powerful impact. No matter what you face, roll up your sleeves and keep going.

➢ Loving who you are plays a vital part in walking in your divine purpose. If you don't love yourself and believe in yourself, then those emotions will bleed into your life and dictate how or if you pursue after your purpose. If you aren't sure of who you are, and you don't have a strong conviction in what you are pursuing then you will be hesitant about walking in your purpose. Begin to build yourself inwardly so that you can be thoroughly equipped to fulfill your divine assignment. Remember, purpose is calling your name......answer the call.

Here is an acronym of the word "PURPOSE" that I created in January 2017.

Prepare: You can begin preparation for your purpose through prayer. Taking the time to acknowledge God will give you the guidance you need to prepare for your purpose. Have a meeting/consultation with God because He has great plans for your life (Proverbs 3:5-6). Take the necessary preparation time to equip you for your purpose. You may know what you're supposed to accomplish, but preparation time is essential so that you have all your ducks in a row before you begin moving forward. Even before Queen Esther was selected as Queen, there was a time of preparation to purify herself before she got an opportunity to go before the King. Prepare yourself. Proverbs 24:27: *"Prepare thy work without, and make it fit for thyself in the field; and afterwards build thine house."* Think about this, what are you preparing for? What preparations are you making NOW for your purpose?

Understanding: Make sure you have a CLEAR understanding of what your purpose is so you don't become easily distracted with things that have nothing to do with your purpose begin to arise. *Proverbs 4:7: "Wisdom is the principal thing; therefore get wisdom: and with all thy getting get understanding."* Distractions will come, but understanding your purpose will help you to stand firm in the midst of them. Are you clear about what you want to accomplish? Do you have a clear understanding of what it will take to walk in your purpose?

Responsible (Responsibility): Walking in your purpose will require you to be responsible. You must be willing to be responsible over the divine assignment that God will have you on. You must be responsible when it comes to going after your business, writing a book, securing a new career. Be a good steward over what God has entrusted into your hands.

Persevere: Persevere is defined from the Merriam-Webster dictionary is: *"Steadfastness in doing something despite difficulty or delay in achieving success."* There are going to be times when you will face opposition as you pursue after your purpose, but you must persevere beyond the opposition. You must stand strong and boldly move towards your destiny. Don't allow the opposition to cause you to derail from your purpose.

Opportunities: When you know your purpose and you walk in it, it creates doors of opportunities to open for you. Proverbs 18:16: *"A man's GIFT maketh room for him, and bringeth him before great men."* God has strategically placed something (gift/purpose) inside of you that can open doors for you. What opportunities are you preparing for? What opportunities have you missed? What will you do now to prevent from missing "the opportunity of a lifetime?"

Seize It: Go after your purpose intentionally. "I meant to do that." Meet the mark; hit the goal....on purpose. Take bold and courageous moves towards your purpose. Don't just talk about what you're going to do, but take the initiative to get it done.

Separate: During your journey towards walking in your purpose, you may need to separate yourself from people who don't believe in you or in where you're going. Your connections affect you in many ways so be mindful of who you hook up with. Everybody can't go where you're going. And that's okay. That destination is set just for you. Take a moment to review Acts 13:1-2 – Saul and Barnabas was separated on purpose for a purpose.

Experience It: Live in your purpose. Embrace it and experience it. Don't be afraid of it.....walk in it. Begin to thrive in all areas of your life. Joseph in the Bible lived in his purpose and experienced it so that he would be in position to save his family. Experiencing your purpose will position you for something greater.

There is an amazing plan for your life. Go after it. Embrace it. Walk in it.

Final Words

Now that you've read through the previous chapters of this book, you should have had an opportunity to dig deep within the inner woman so that you could experience the healing from the inside out. Taking time to answer the questions and writing your innermost thoughts signifies that you value your worth. Now that you have processed your experiences, thoughts and emotions, you can now allow that inner healing to push forth outwardly for others to see. You are ready to bring out the best you ever.

In case you didn't know, you were originally created for greatness. God ordained it to be so. He had a strategic plan to formulate the best you. Along the way, you were faced with obstacles that may have been hard, but guess what you made it through. Those obstacles were not meant to destroy you, but God has and will continue to use them to develop and expose the greatness within.

No longer must you settle for mediocre living or accept the negativity of others concerning your past. No longer must you underestimate the greatness within you. No longer must you allow others to devalue your worth. No more room for low self-esteem, it's time to recognize who you are and love who you are…..right now. Allow the truth of God's Word and all He says about you to be poured into your heart. It's a new day my dear, Sister. It's time for the new you, the changed you, the healed you to spring forth. Embrace the newness.

You are God's workmanship and His masterpiece. You possess power and greatness. You are destined for greatness. I know the naysayers are telling you differently, but they are called naysayers because all they know to say is negative things. They are strategically placed in your life to frustrate the purpose for your very existence, but don't waste time allowing their words to distract you. Don't let their words, their actions or lack thereof take you off course. Greatness, greater days and greater blessings are awaiting your arrival. Move towards the greater with vitality.

As Rafiki said in Lion King, "It is time." Yes, it is time to re-launch the new you! She's been hidden for some time because of all the things you've experienced, but the woman that God destined for you to be must emerge. You are the woman who loves who she is from the inside out. You might have been overlooked, underestimated or rejected in the past, but it's time to fast forward into your greater days. Your latter shall be greater than your former! Yes, I'm talking to you. It's a new day and a new season.

No more sad days. No more days of feeling depressed or overwhelmed. Take a deep breath. Breathe in and out. Guess what? You're ALIVE! You made it through and now it is time to shine.

Take what you've learned from the words written in this book. They were specifically meant to minister to your heart from mine.....well even from the heart of God as I listened for His instructions. He had you in mind. He always has you in mind. He has a plan just for you and I'm telling you it's great. You got to believe that for yourself. Allow God to pour His love in you. Allow God the opportunity to show you what He has for your life. It will simply amaze you. It's your time. It's your season to shine. You better recognize!

Love yourself and LIVE!

About the Author

Stephanie L. McKenny is a native of Montclair, New Jersey. She received her license to preach in August 1993 in Newark, NJ. She assists her husband in ministry where she serves in various capacities. Stephanie McKenny has three children and four grandchildren. She is a graduate of Columbia College. She continued her graduate students at Webster University for a Masters in Mental Health Counseling. She is the author of nine books. Her latest books are: *"Better than That"* and *"Got to Do Better,"* which are teen novels. Better than That was adapted into a teen stage play production. Stephanie McKenny can be contacted via email, website and social media: slmckenny@gmail.com, her website address is: www.stephaniemckennny.com. She is also on Facebook and Instagram

If you would like to book Stephanie L. McKenny for a speaking engagement, book signing, workshop/book discussion, you may do so by emailing her at: slmckenny@gmail.com and/or making a written request through mail to: P.O. Box 291205, Columbia, SC 29229

Additional Reflections

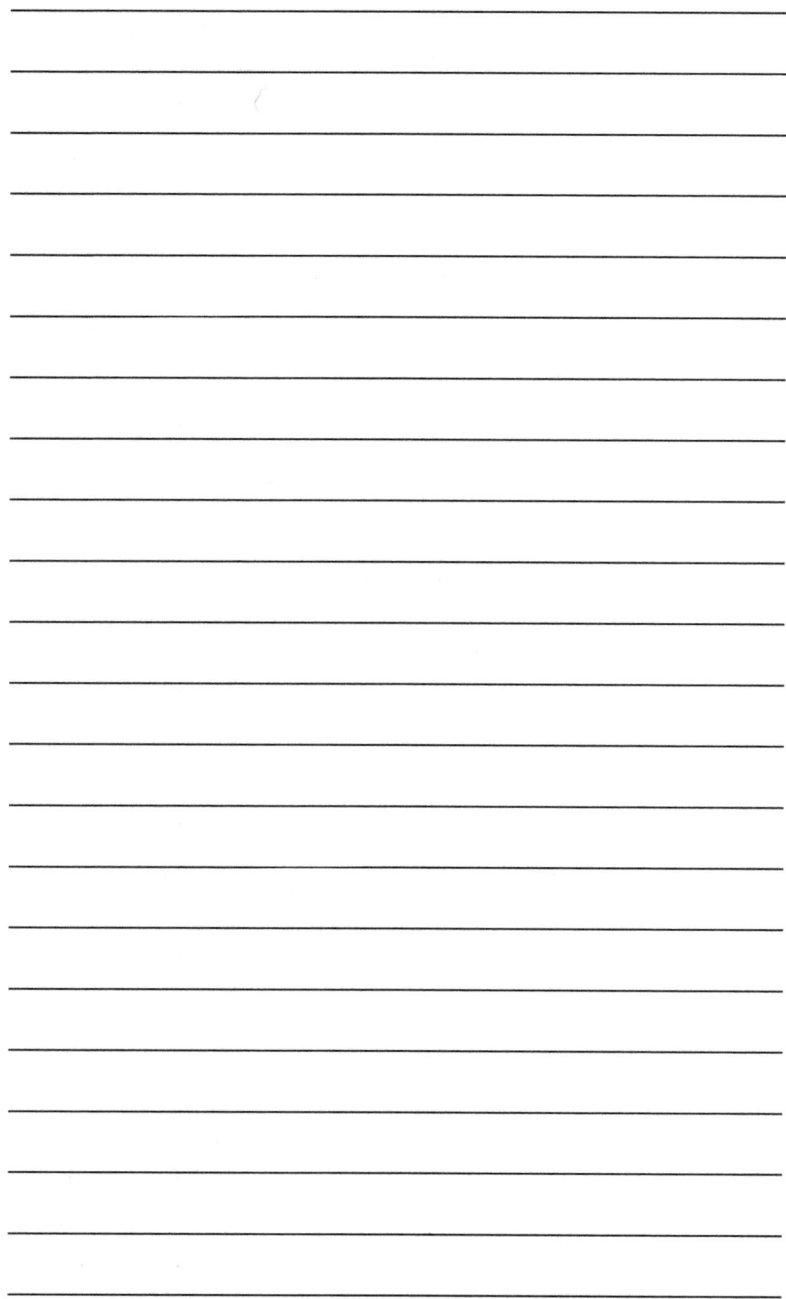

www.ingramcontent.com/pod-product-compliance
Lightning Source LLC
Chambersburg PA
CBHW062000040426
42447CB00010B/1838